God Makes Our World

Carolyn Byers

REVIEW AND HERALD® PUBLISHING ASSOCIATION
WASHINGTON, DC 20039-0555
HAGERSTOWN, MD 21740

The author assumes full responsibility for the accuracy of all facts and quotations as cited in this book.

This book was
Edited by Penny Estes Wheeler
Art direction by Linda Anderson McDonald and Stephen Hall
Cover art and direction by Paul Turnbaugh
Cover design by Stephen Hall
Typeset: Palatino 12 pt.

PRINTED IN U.S.A.

R&H Cataloging Service
Byers, Carolyn.
    Forever stories.
    5 v.

    1. Bible stories, English.   I. Title.

    BS2401.B74   1989

ISBN 10: 0-8280-0502-8
ISBN 13: 978-0-8280-0502-9

Visit us at **www.reviewandherald.com** for information on other Review and Herald® products.

for
Brenda, Branton, Brady,
and Brani

Contents

The Shiniest Angel

A long, long time ago God lived with His Son and the angels in heaven.

Heaven was a happy place. The angels sang while they worked. Each angel had his own special work. Some stood at the gates to welcome visitors. Others carried messages.

Lucifer, the shiniest angel of all, stood next to God. He was God's special helper. Every angel liked the work God gave him. To obey the One they loved brought each angel joy.

Each day God invited the angels to meet with Him. Every angel arrived on time. Not one wanted to miss even the first song. Lucifer, the most glorious angel of all, sang a note to start the music. All the thousands and thousands of angels joined him. They sang:

"Holy, holy, holy, is the Lord God Almighty, who was and is and is to come . . ." *

Then the angels knelt to thank God for making heaven so pretty. They thanked God for giving them a happy life.

God and His Son loved Their happy home with the angels. But Their love was so big that They wanted somebody new to love. They talked together and decided to make a brand-new world.

Their new world would have sweet-smelling flowers and tall green trees. It would have deep rivers and bubbling streams. The new world would be alive with buzzing bees, trilling birds, and warm, fuzzy animals. It would be happy because people would live there, too. People would be like a family to God and His Son.

*Revelation 4:8, RSV

It made God and His Son smile to
think about people. The people would laugh
and sing and play. They would think up new
ideas. God would enjoy talking to them. God's new
people would be kind and loving to each other and to
the animals. Then joy would ripple from their world
to other worlds.

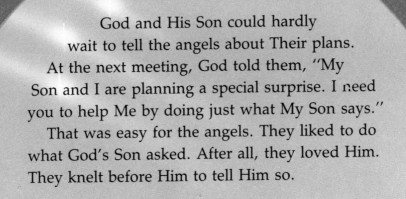

God and His Son could hardly
wait to tell the angels about Their plans.
At the next meeting, God told them, "My
Son and I are planning a special surprise. I need
you to help Me by doing just what My Son says."
That was easy for the angels. They liked to do
what God's Son asked. After all, they loved Him.
They knelt before Him to tell Him so.

One angel, however, frowned at God's words. He walked away from his place next to God. This angel was Lucifer, the shiniest angel.

"So God is making a new world," he said to himself. "He didn't ask me about it. I am the smartest and most beautiful of all the angels. Why should God expect me to obey His Son? He is selfish. Humph! I know I can do things better than He can. If I were in charge, everything would be fine."

Lucifer's eyes grew dark and mean. "God is not good. He is making a bad mistake."

Lucifer asked all the angels to come to a secret meeting. He stood up to talk to them.

"Because I love you, I must tell you something," he said.

He smiled. He wanted the angels to believe him. "With God's Son in charge, our freedom is gone. He will tell us what to do. We are angels. We don't need that Son to boss us around."

Lucifer shook his fist. "I'll never again honor God's Son. I won't obey Him either. If you are smart, you'll do as I do," he shouted. "I love you more than God's Son does. I love you more than God does. Let me be your God."

After the meeting, the angels talked together in small groups. "What is happening to us?" they asked each other. "What has gone wrong? Why don't we feel like singing?"

Most of the angels felt afraid. One hurried to tell God what had happened. He found God talking with His Son about Lucifer. The angel listened. "Lucifer is ruined," he heard Them say. "Lucifer will always make trouble."

The angel thought about God's words. What should They do with Lucifer? Should They kill the shiniest angel? If Lucifer died, then the other angels in heaven might be afraid of God and His Son. Many angels would wonder, Who was right? Who really was the better leader? Who really loved them more? Who was the good one? Was it God, or Lucifer?

All heaven was upset. Some of the angels cried. They wondered, What will happen? Will God still want to make a new world?

Then an angel messenger arrived. "We're having a meeting," he said. "Everyone should come quickly."

The angels hurried to the meeting. They listened quietly while God talked. "My Son and I will still make a new world. And I still want you to do what He says. Just as you do what I tell you to do."

Many angels turned to look at Lucifer. His eyes were angry. His face did not look happy. He shook his head as God spoke.

God's voice was sad. "Since Lucifer will not obey My Son, he cannot stay in heaven."

Lucifer jumped up. "Your rules are bad. No one can obey them!" he shouted. "We don't need Your rules."

He pointed to his many angel friends. "All these angels are with me," he said. "Will you make them leave heaven, too?

"I am going to stay here. I am going to be the boss. And we're ready to fight!"

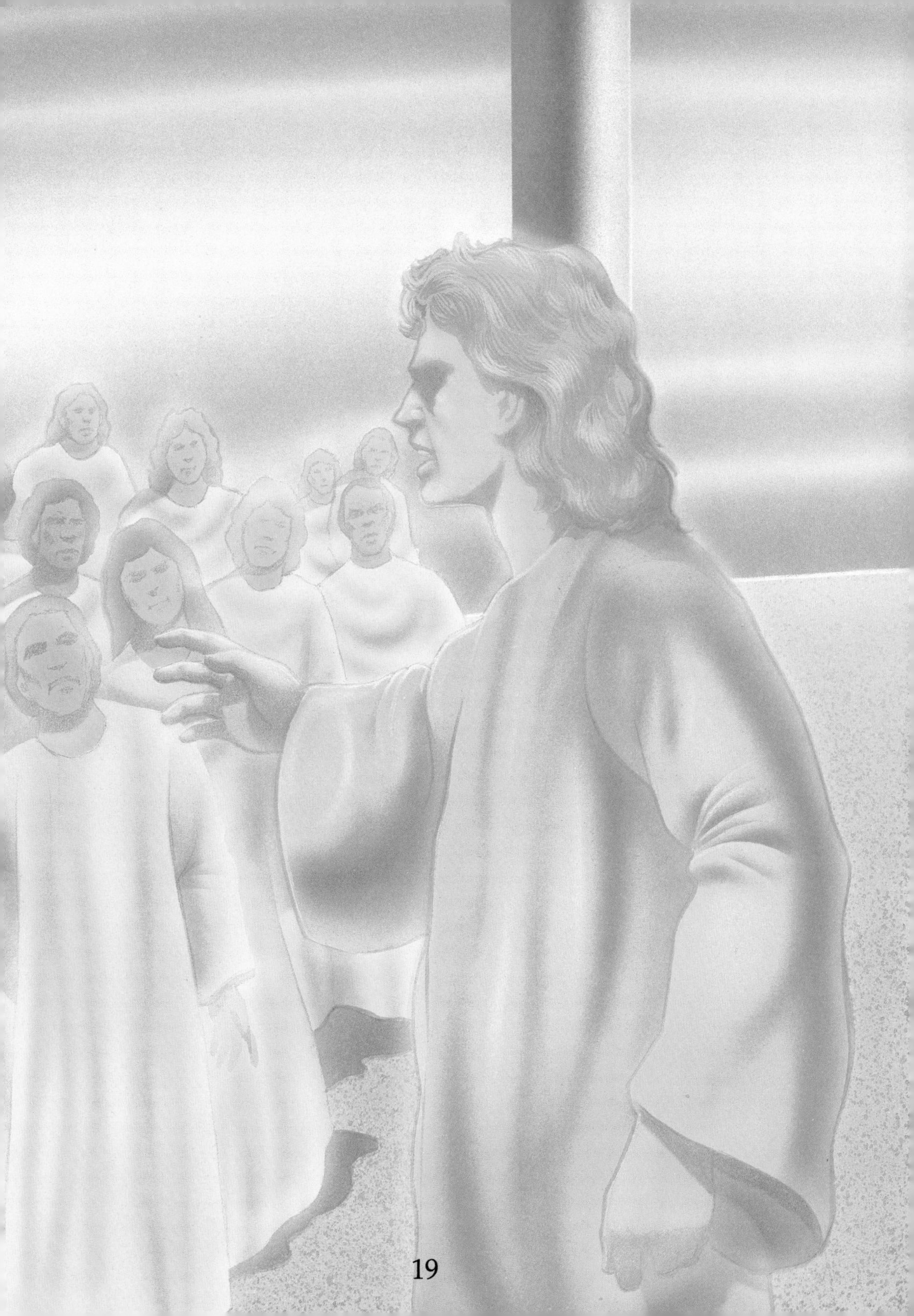

Then there was war in heaven. Lucifer and his friends
were pushed out. Afterwards, heaven's gates were locked.

Heaven seemed too quiet with many of the angels gone.
At worship time, the music was softer. Many beautiful
voices were missing. Tears trickled down some of the
angels' faces. They longed for their friends.

Again God talked with His Son about making a new
world. Would They let Lucifer go to the new world? Would
They let him talk to God's new people? What if
people—God's new children—chose to follow the shiniest
angel? What then?

God and His Son talked about happiness. What
would bring everyone everywhere happiness for all
time? They decided that people should be able to choose
whom they wanted to obey. To help them choose, people
ould be told about Lucifer. God would tell His new
ildren that Lucifer would make them sad and sick. And if
ey chose to obey Lucifer, he would make them die.
"We must let Lucifer talk to them," God said. "That is
r. But We will not let him follow them around. Lucifer
n talk to them only when they go near one spot, the
bidden tree."
"What will happen if people listen to Lucifer?" an
gel asked.
God and His Son knew what would happen.
ople would hurt each other. Lucifer
uld make people sick. The beautiful
v world would be filled with mean,
people.
'Then what happens if one child
ides he doesn't like Lucifer?" the
els wanted to know. "What
pens if someone wants to be
de kind and good again?"
God and His Son thought
plan.

A New World

God's big voice called into the darkness. "Let there be light."

The deep blackness melted away so all could see what God would make.

The evening and the morning were the first day of the new world.

"Let there be sky and air to breathe," God said. His voice sounded like music.

God knew living things would need air.

That evening and morning were the second day.

God spoke again. "Let there be land here and water over there."

It happened just as He said it should. Land was here and water there.

Then God called out, "Let Us make the land pretty with trees and flowers."

God looked at the pansies and lilies. He looked at the apricot and cherry trees. "This is good," He said. "I like it."

And the evening and the morning were the third day.

On the fourth day God spoke
again. "Let a yellow moon brighten the
night. Let the starlight of a billion stars show
the passing of time. And let a round golden sun
warm the world in daytime."

That evening the moon and stars shone in the
sky. The next morning the sun rose on a quiet
world.

And the evening and the morning were the
fourth day.

But sunrises seem more beautiful when birds
are singing. God broke the silence when He said,
"Let there be birds in the air."

Suddenly the earth vibrated with the calls
of eagles and cardinals and crows and
canaries.

Then God said, "Let there be
creatures in the sea."

In that moment, dolphins arched above deep water. In rivers, sunlight glinted off the colors of a rainbow trout. And in the streams, minnows and crayfish played tag.

"Let the birds and fish have babies," God said.

In the seas, mother fish and father fish darted about. Each pair was looking for a place to raise their family.

A mother duck started building her nest near some reeds. She lined it with grass and leaves. Then she added her own down-feathers for a pillow. She was ready for her eggs.

And the evening and the morning were the fifth day.

On the sixth day God said, "Let there be animals. We want animals that say 'Moo, moo' and animals that say 'Woof, woof.' We want an animal with a long, long neck. We want a silly animal that hangs by its tail.

"Let there be animals that people can ride. And there shall be soft animals for children to hold and cuddle.

"All the animals are to have babies that look just like them. Baby kittens will grow up to be cats. Baby lambs will grow up to look like their mommies and daddies."

The angels looked at all the creatures God had made. "Each one is lovely," they agreed.

They waited, expecting something else. "When will God make people?" they asked each other.

Finally the time came.

God knelt down on the ground. With His own hands, God shaped a big man. He formed two long legs. He made elbows and fingers. He molded the nose and lips.

Then God bent down and breathed life into His man. The man awoke and sat up.

God named him Adam.

God put Adam to work on the very first day. He asked Adam to name the animals. Adam started right away.

Adam looked over a humpbacked animal. "Its name is Camel," he said. He saw a big spotted animal. "That one will be Leopard," he said. "And the big one with the stripes, I'll name Tiger."

Then he noticed a little animal with long ears and a fluffy tail. Adam smiled. "That animal will be called Rabbit," he said.

When Adam called their names, the animals came running. They knew Adam was their master.

While naming the animals, Adam noticed the animals came in twos. There were two two dogs, two elephants, two beavers. "Why ere only one of me?" he asked God. "Where is my r one?"

It God hadn't forgotten. God planned something wonderful Adam's very first day.

wedding.

God made the wedding happen like a beautiful dream. God let Adam fall asleep. Then he took a rib from Adam's side and made a woman.

When Adam woke up, there she was. Her name was Eve. Adam loved her at once.

God said to Adam, "I want you to love her and her children as you love yourself. Do you want to do that?"

Adam smiled. "Yes, I do."

To Eve, God said, "I want you to love Adam and his children as you love yourself. Do you want to do that?"

She nodded. "Yes, I do."

That busy evening and morning were the sixth day.

One, two, three, four, five, six days God worked. On the seventh evening God and His Son looked at the brand-new world. It was very good.

God didn't make anything on the seventh day. He just enjoyed the new world, the new animals, and the new people He had made. It was such a happy day that God blessed it.

God said, "Let the seventh day be a holy day. It will give My children time to spend with me. I want them to remember when their world was made. So at the close of every week let there be a holiday."

Adam and Eve had a wonderful time with God on the seventh day.

God's Park

On that very first Sabbath God gave the newlyweds a tour of their new home. It wasn't a marble palace like kings live in. It wasn't a farmhouse or an ocean cottage. It wasn't an apartment house or a mobile home. It was a park.

God led Adam and Eve through the park. Eve sniffed the sweet air. She took a deep breath. "Adam," she whispered. "What is it I smell?"

"It is a magnolia tree," he said. "You will like the pine trees, too. I will show you the pine grove later."

They walked on a path that edged a silvery river. Ducks floated along beside them. Fish darted beneath the surface of the water.

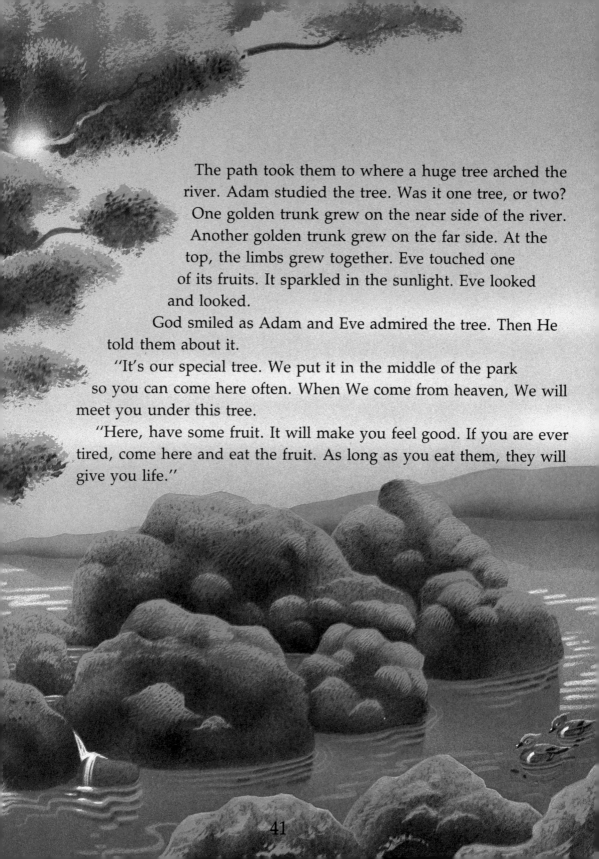

The path took them to where a huge tree arched the river. Adam studied the tree. Was it one tree, or two? One golden trunk grew on the near side of the river. Another golden trunk grew on the far side. At the top, the limbs grew together. Eve touched one of its fruits. It sparkled in the sunlight. Eve looked and looked.

God smiled as Adam and Eve admired the tree. Then He told them about it.

"It's our special tree. We put it in the middle of the park so you can come here often. When We come from heaven, We will meet you under this tree.

"Here, have some fruit. It will make you feel good. If you are ever tired, come here and eat the fruit. As long as you eat them, they will give you life."

Under the tree, God told them, "I love you. My Son loves you. All th
angels in heaven love you. We want to take care of you. Do you love u:

Adam said, "I do."

Eve said, "I do, too."

God told them that to be happy, they must obey Him. "Will you obe
Me?" He asked.

"I will obey You," Adam said. Eve said, "I want to obey, too."

"Do you see that big tree over there?" God asked. He pointed to a fine tree.

They nodded.

"That tree belongs to an enemy," God told them. "The enemy can only harm you if you go to that tree. If you don't go near it, you will be safe."

God looked sad and serious. Adam and Eve had never seen Him look that way. "You must never, never, go near that tree. You must never eat any fruit from that tree," He said. "If you eat from that tree, I will know that you have chosen the enemy to care for you. But he is bad. He will make you die."

God looked at Adam and Eve. "Adam, you help Eve. Eve, you help Adam. You can eat from all the other trees. Only leave that one tree alone. Do you understand?"

They nodded their heads.

In the days that followed, Adam and Eve explored their new home. Little paths wound in and out of the vines and trees. Adam and Eve never knew what they might find. They peeked under bushes and found little frogs blinking back at them.

Adam climbed a tall tree to look at a nest. "Eve. Come, see! Look at the baby woodpeckers," he called.

"Oh, they are adorable," Eve said. She pointed to the flower she wore in her hair. "Now you must come see the lilies that I found."

Adam followed his wife. "Oh, they're pretty," he said.

The two lovers adored their park home. They slept under the stars every night. There was nothing to fear. The bears and tigers and snakes were their friends. There were no stinging bees or biting ants to harm them.

God had asked them to care for the park. So they spent part of every day, except Sabbath, working. Sometimes they clipped and arranged the vines to make bowers for shade.

"I'll snip this grape branch here," Adam said. "Then we can plant another grapevine across from it. When the vines grow larger, I'll build a trellis for them to climb."

Adam and Eve worked together. Whenever a plant in the park grew a tiny new seedling, Adam dug it up. Eve helped him find a new spot where it could grow and look pretty.

When God made His park, He saved a spot of ground where Adam could grow food. God gave Adam seeds to plant in the ground. Each seed grew a surprise—corn, beans, oats, watermelon, and papaya. When the food was ripe, Adam and Eve picked and ate it. God knew that they would enjoy their food more if they could help grow it.

Angels visited Adam and Eve as they worked and played. The angels taught them songs to sing and told them stories. Adam and Eve listened to the angel stories about heaven and God.

"God doesn't want us to go near that one tree," Adam and Eve told the angels one day.

"God is right," the angels said. "Lucifer lived in heaven. But he hated God's Son because Lucifer wanted to be God. Then he started a war. Lucifer and his friends were pushed out of heaven.

"Now Lucifer wants to tell you that God is bad. God will let him talk to you, but only at that one tree. He can only talk to you if you choose to listen."

The angels' faces looked very serious. They wanted Adam and Eve to listen carefully.

"If you love God," they said, "you will stay away from that tree."

One of the angels sighed. "Lucifer is not called Lucifer any more. He is not shiny and pretty any more. Now he is called Satan. Satan means 'enemy.' Satan is our enemy!

"Don't ever, ever, ever go near the forbidden tree. Satan will tell you lies. But God is always truthful. Satan will make you want to fight. But God has made this garden for you so you can always live in peace. Satan's ways lead to death. But God's way is the way of happiness. Satan will force you to follow him. But God gives you the freedom to choose. Only you can make the decision."

Two Trees

For some time Adam and Eve enjoyed the park that God had made for them. They hummed as they worked. Sometimes they ran just for the joy of it. They laughed and played with the animals.

In the cool of the evenings, God and His Son often came to the park to visit Adam and Eve. They walked together. They talked quietly. Later, as Adam and Eve worked around the park, they thought about the things God told them.

One day, though, everything changed. On that day, Eve wandered away from Adam. Maybe she was gathering fruit to fix for dinner. Maybe she was following a new pathway. But suddenly she found herself near the tree that God had warned them to stay away from.

She might not have noticed the tree except that a voice called to her from its branches. Looking up in surprise, she saw a snake among the leaves. It had wings and looked like a big sparkling butterfly.

The snake spoke sweetly. "Did God tell you that you couldn't eat from *all* the trees?"

We can eat from all except one," Eve said. "He has told us that if we eat from this tree, we will die."

Eve had seen snakes before, but they had never talked. She didn't guess that Satan, the enemy, was tricking her. She didn't guess that Satan was making the snake talk. Eve thought of turning away. But she chose to stay.

"You're beautiful, Eve," the snake told her. "You're smart, too. God knows that if you eat from this tree, you will be like Him. You will know both good and evil. You won't die."

The butterfly-snake took a bite from the fruit. Eve watched it eat. The fruit smelled wonderful.

As Eve stood there, she had to think. She had to choose
whom she would believe. Should she believe God? Or should
she believe the beautiful talking snake?

The snake handed her a piece of fruit. Quickly Eve decided.
She chose to believe the snake. She took the fruit and ate it. It
tasted good, so she picked some more to share with Adam.

As soon as Adam saw the fruit, he knew Satan had given it to Eve. He knew he should not eat it. Adam looked at his lovely wife and thought, *If I do not eat the fruit, maybe God will take Eve away.* The thought made him lonely. He was afraid.

Now it was Adam's turn to choose. Whom did he love more—God or Eve?

Then Adam decided. He grabbed the fruit and ate it.

Satan, the enemy angel, laughed and laughed and laughed.

"Ha! Ha! Ha! The people God made are all mine! Their pretty world is mine. The animals are mine."

Satan's smile looked sly and horrible. "Just wait until Adam and Eve get to God's tree of life. They will eat more fruit and suffer a much longer time."

God and His Son knew what was happening. All the angels in heaven knew what was happening. It made them weep. God quickly sent angels to guard the tree of life.

God came to the park that evening as He often did. Always before His children had waited eagerly for Him to come. This time, though, they were hiding. Far from the tree of life God found two sorry-looking people.

Adam and Eve had the sure signs of Satan's disease. They were cold and shivering. They were so afraid they did not even want to talk to God, their best friend.

Besides that, Adam and Eve were fighting. Adam was growling at Eve. "Why did you take off and leave me? How could you obey that snake? What was wrong with you?"

"What's the problem?" God asked Adam.

He answered, "Eve gave me the fruit to eat."

Then God asked Eve, "What happened?"

She pointed toward the forbidden tree. "The snake tricked me and I ate the fruit."

God then spoke to the snake. "From now on, you will not have wings. You will crawl in the dust." His voice grew stronger and He pointed at Satan. "*You* made the snake talk. Even though you fight, someday you will be destroyed."

God looked sadly at Eve. His voice was ever so gentle. "Now it will hurt when you have babies."

He turned to Adam. His voice was full of tears. "I didn't want you to know about evil. Now you will know what evil means. It will be hard to grow the food you eat. You will get hot and sweaty when you work. Then you will grow old and die."

Then God made coats for Adam and Eve. The coats felt warm.

Then God told Adam and Eve to leave the pretty park. He knew that they wouldn't be happy there for they would be afraid of God. Adam and Eve would never enjoy walking with Him again. Now they must live outside the gate with Satan.

It made God very sad to put Adam and Eve out of their pretty home.

Eve wept for she didn't want to leave. Adam took one last look at his garden. Some food looked ready to eat. But he couldn't pick it. Adam and Eve walked through the gate. When they were outside, angels stood in the doorway. They would guard it so that Adam and Eve could not eat from the tree of life.

Only one thing made Adam and Eve feel better. They remembered that God had a special plan for them.